INSTANT CALMNESS

Follow your dreams. They know the way!

Love,
mom

Instant Calmness

The INSTANT-Series *Presents*

INSTANT

CALMNESS

How to Calm Down and Stay Calm in Any Tough Situation Instantly!

Instant Series Publication

Copyright © Instant Series Publication

All rights reserved.

It is impermissible to reproduce any part of this book without prior consent. All violations will be prosecuted to the fullest extent of the law.

While attempts have been made to verify the information contained within this publication, neither the author nor the publisher assumes any responsibility for errors, omissions, interpretation or usage of the subject matter herein.

This publication contains the opinions and ideas of its author and is intended for informational purpose only. The author and publisher shall in no event held liable for any loss or other damages incurred from the usage of this publication.

ISBN 978-1-517-37577-5

Printed in the United States of America

First Edition

FIRST STEP:

Before proceeding, visit http://www.instantseries.com, and join the **INSTANT Newsletter** now.

You will want to! :)

Instant Calmness

CONTENTS

Chapter 1 - The Quest and Reward for Claiming Calmness in Your Life

11 - The Storm Before The Calm

13 - Steer From The Chaos

15 - The Ultimate Inner Self-Control

17 - Exercise: Block Out The Noise

19 - The PET Technique

21 - Awaken Your Zen

Chapter 2 - Control Your Perceived Environmental Reality

23 - ESP (Environmental Sensory Perception)

25 - How To Create Your Own Fortress Of Solitude

29 - Call Forth Your Fortress

30 - Exercise: Build Your Peaceful Palace

Chapter 3 - Release All Negativities through Transference

32 - Energy In The Palm

33 - Tension Transference Technique

35 - Exercise: Negativity Demolition

Chapter 4 - Pause the World Around You
38 - Shutdown Mode
41 - Exercise: Letting Go

Chapter 5 - Refresh and Stay Fresh
42 - Get To Neutral
43 - Exercise: Keep The Day At Bay
44 - Exercise: Neutralize When Needed

Chapter 6 - Calm Yourself
47 - Exercise 1: Refresh Your Mood
47 - Exercise 2: Shutdown And Respite
48 - Exercise 3: Environmental Takeover
49 - Exercise 4: Goodbye Tension

Chapter 7 - Peace Treaty with Yourself
51 - Achieve Peace At Last
52 - Maintain Peace

Instant Calmness

Instant Calmness

Chapter 1

The Quest and Reward for Claiming Calmness in Your Life

The Storm Before The Calm

For many of us, our lives are characterized by too much noise, too much work, too many demands on our time and money. We seem to be bombarded with responsibilities and restraints left and right - no matter where we turn.

Does this sound all too familiar?

What many of us want or, to be honest, actually need, is a little calmness within our lives.

Calmness, for most people, has become an illusion what with all the chaos, distractions, and stress that we deal with daily. It's not that anyone chooses to live like a popcorn kernel about to pop, but, for reasons that appear outside of a person's control, they just kind of have to convince themselves that this is something normal, something they just have to *"learn to live with."*

<u>Newsflash</u>: There's nothing "normal" about it.

Maybe you believe you have to "live with it" for professional reasons or family reasons, that there's nothing you can do about it.

But why would anyone want to continue living like that? Who wants to remain engulfed in daily worries and frustrations? *Well, nobody!*

Calmness is attainable, and you need to channel in on it.

Steer From The Chaos

Generally, we tend to think of "calmness" as something produced by our **environment**. If it's quiet outside, nobody around to bother you, you must be experiencing calmness, right? But this produces an instant problem...

- How can you control the crowded 7:00 a.m. drive to work when someone cuts you off in bumper to bumper traffic? How do you control *your environment* when it's comprised of different people with different personalities and the unforeseen situations that continually sneak up on you?

You can't. Traffic, work, errands, your boss—these are all part of a seemingly endless list of things that drive you crazy but are mostly outside of your control.

You can only control your reaction to it.

To tell you the truth, it would be impossible to control all environmental factors all the time. Even if you've succeeded in controlling 50% of the factors preventing you from exploding in a fit of rage, the other 50% would represent those factors that are simply part of the unchangeable facts of life. Trying to maintain a "stress-free" environment is…liable to drive you crazy.

Thus, the goal here is to **achieve calmness**, no matter what the environment or situation. By mastering your mental reflexes you can gain control over your emotional response in any situation.

For example, instead of letting uncertainty fill you with fear, or letting a worry over a tough decision control your attitude, your mental reflexes can actually help you distance yourself from these pressures and view them objectively. This means you'll be able to ignore the pressure and take your time, doing more without worrying over potential mistakes. When you let pressure drive and control you, you end up with a badly finished job or a mediocre performance.

In essence, you've stilted your abilities by obsessing over every detail for fear it will come back to haunt you.

A calm person doesn't let imagined fears and worries take over his or her performance. They can take time to see what needs to be done, and then do it thoroughly and well, without hesitation and without uncertainty.

Calmness allows you to better *utilize* your abilities and *neutralize* negativity right away.

The Ultimate Inner Self-Control

Now let's take to the courtroom to illustrate a point.

> A judge is faced with numerous criminals every day, and he has to be able to keep himself calm in any situation he's confronted with. He has to view every case with calm and detachment, keeping his personal

preferences removed from the case so that the prisoner is ensured an unbiased trial.

He also has to deal with all sorts of drama. No criminal who receives a heavy sentence is going to take it rationally, and he's definitely not going to take it pleasantly. The judge has sit through all of this, maintaining order in the courtroom and upholding the proper dignity that the law deserves. If he loses his self-control and lowers himself to the criminal's level in order to argue with him, he loses all the respect and authority that his position, and the law, demands.

You have to remember that a judge faces stressful situations on a regular basis. If he allowed himself to be fazed by every case, it wouldn't take long for him to become an emotional wreck.

This comparison extends to us all. We have to be able to keep calm in any situation. If you allowed every stressful or unpleasant incident to affect you, you'd end up an emotional mess.

You have to be able to train yourself to react calmly. In essence, you're like the judge. You have to be detached enough to decide what is the right course of action in any situation. When you've done the right thing, you have nothing to worry about. The rest is not your problem, and you can just move on.

<u>Exercise</u>: Block Out The Noise

As an <u>exercise</u>, let's see how adept you are at managing your mind in a distracting or stressful environment.

1.) Find yourself a place in your house (such as in your living room with the TV on) or somewhere public (such as a crowded gathering) where there's plenty of noise.

2.) Grab a piece of paper and try to write out a description of what you did during the day. Concentrate *only* on writing.

3.) Do your best to take your time and isolate the noise and distractions from your mind. To do this, you're going to have to concentrate hard on what you're going to write, then actually put down those exact words.

4.) Don't look anywhere else. That paper should become the only object in the right here and right now.

- Were you able to isolate the noise successfully? Explain.

- How long does your concentration last?

- Were you able to write down everything you wanted? Explain.

The point of this exercise is to help you learn to focus on the essentials. Instead of attempting to change your environment, you're training your mind to isolate itself from inevitable disturbances, then project the calmness achieved in your mind into your exterior environment.

The PET Technique

Now, the previous exercise can be time consuming, and - let's face it - you're not always going to be able to sit down and write on a piece of paper to create a lovey-dovey peaceful environment, not to mention the fact that if you haven't had time to master it yet, it's not always a viable option.

So if you can't always do that exercise anytime or anywhere, how do you reach a calming mental state?

Well, let's take this to the next level with the *"peaceful environmental teleportation"* technique, or **PET technique**.

Strange as it may sound, teleportation is the key. No, we're not talking science fiction.

- How about creating that peaceful environment of yours first, then "**anchoring**" it to something <u>you can physically do</u>? That way, whenever you need to, by performing that *simple action*, you can automatically teleport yourself to that environment (like instant mental teleportation).

Still sound a lot like sci-fi? Here's the broken-down explanation.

To use the PET technique, you first have to create an ideal peaceful environment isolated from noise (or even use that previous blocked-out noise environment you worked on in the first exercise), then anchor it to a **physical movement** you can use to teleport yourself to that place.

For instance, if you *snap your finger* or *clap your hand* after you've preprogrammed this associated movement as an "anchor" to that environment, you'll mentally teleport yourself back to that aura of calm in that peaceful environment.

Don't sweat the petty stuffs. PET the sweaty stuffs. :)

Try it!

Awaken Your Zen

When you really think about it, the idea of "calmness" is rather like the **concept of Zen**. But what does "Zen" mean? Do you have to become a hippie to fully embrace it?

No, not at all. *You only need to live in the present.*

Once you've dealt with past mistakes, you can't dwell on them. That's the easiest way to negatively impact your present performance.

Nor can you dwell on the future. The future is so uncertain that focusing on it is only going to cripple you here and now. You can *prepare* for the future, but once you've done that, the only thing you can do is put it out of your mind.

So keep the Zen principle in mind as you do all the exercises from here on out. Remember, these exercises have been designed to help you deal with and live in the present, because you can't achieve calmness in the past or the future, only in the present.

Chapter 2

Control Your Perceived Environmental Reality

ESP (Environmental Sensory Perception)

It's well-known that **surroundings** can have a major effect on mood and performance. Décor (colors, paintings, furniture, etc.), the airing and size of the room, coffee ready-made in the cafeteria; all these things can impact your mood.

For instance, if you're in love with your furnishings at work, you love the smell of fresh coffee that always awaits you in the morning, or you enjoy interacting with your awesome co-workers, chances are that waking up every morning and driving to work is no big sacrifice.

But ultimately, these are pretty ideal circumstances, because not everybody can get the perfect view even at the 5 star hotels.

You're more likely to run into places where maybe the horrible décor, cluttered spaces, or less than sociable companions, all add tension to your mood. You may simply be a worker, a visitor, or a patient, but you have to put up with it anyway. But it's just not welcoming, and all you want to do is get the heck out of there.

On the other hand, there are places that can immediately relieve your tension and can even help you forget that you were angry or stressed about something in the first place.

Wouldn't it be amazing to be able to feel like you were in an ideal place even in the waiting room at the DMV? What if you were told that there were ways to actually reproduce these sensations whenever you wanted?

You can't always control your environment, but you can always control your perception of it.

How To Create Your Own Fortress Of Solitude

Even if you live with high levels of stress, chances are you have that one special place, a place where all of your problems seem to disappear the minute you step in.

Here's where we build a little more on the "ideal environment" mentioned before.

This method is very similar to the "PET technique" discussed earlier and actually ties in very closely. You're using your mind to reproduce particular settings, colors, even scents, that you find calming and stress-relieving.

This is also where the Zen principle comes in, because this exercise helps you achieve that ability to "live in the moment" that is so important to Zen philosophy. It helps you regain your calm and take full control of your senses again. And just like anything else, the more you practice the easier it'll be for you to effectively apply this method.

> STEP 1: The first thing you have to do in order to recreate your calming environment is to put all the details together. (You can even write it down half an hour or so before you'll actually be using the exercise.) But you're obviously not going to be able to remember every specific detail, so the thing to do is to identify between 5 and 8 **dominant characteristics** - the ones that have the most powerful effect on your mood. It may be the colors, the furniture, the airiness or outdoorsy feel, the overriding scent (air-fresheners, coffee, cleaning products, etc.) - whichever aspects most reflect stability and peace, even in a rough or constantly changing environment.

STEP 2: The aspects you choose shouldn't even be too closely related. If you can manage it, they should be all different things; that way you have a wider variety of objects, and you'll have a greater chance of being able to match at least one of them with something in your actual physical surroundings. For instance, if one of the items on the list is the sea-green walls of your ideal environment, look for something that contains that color. If your favorite furniture is wooden or metal, try finding something around you that's made of the same material.

See? None of these things are really related, but they all connect you with a sense of harmony and enhance your mood *here and now*.

STEP 3: After you identify these separate items, put them all together in the left half of your mind. Then start moving them to the right half, arranging them however you want them. It'll look a lot like a before-and-after photo. When you're done, visualize the setting as if it was right in front of your eyes. This way you can study it thoroughly and effectively remember the most important details.

STEP 4: Now imagine yourself into the setting. Visualize yourself actually entering the room, feeling the warmth or coolness, smelling the scented freshener… Imagine the actual feel of the chair you sink into. You're making the setting real, if only in your mind. You're living in the moment, learning to feel calm and comfortable in that setting. You are the architect. You're taking control of this place and making it your "fortress of calmness." It's all in your mind, but it's real just the same because it's related to a real feeling, the real calming effect it has on you.

Once you record these details mentally, **your mind can automatically reproduce them**. It reproduces the effects of the details you came up with - the setting, the scent, the colors; they each bring up a comfortable, calming feeling you can call on in stressful situations.

It doesn't matter where you are: it can be the bus stop, the line at the grocery store, the dentist's waiting room - it doesn't matter. As soon as you call up your "personal haven," you're taking complete control, both of that place and of your mood.

Call Forth Your Fortress

Say, for instance, that you're waiting in line at the DMV to renew your license. The queue is long, the people around you are impatient and noisy, and the seats are uncomfortable. Chances are you don't want to be there, the number of people is nerve-racking, and you've got a million other things you need to be doing.

In these situations, it's easy for anyone to lose control to a panic attack or a growing irritability. It doesn't help that most of the time you don't even have the option of getting up and leaving.

This is where you need your "fortress of solitude," aka "calmness."

You should work on creating your ideal environment before your visit, so you can call it up immediately. It's already there for you, so try to mentally transfer yourself into it, and try to really live in this moment of calmness you've created for yourself.

After 5 or 10 minutes, you'll begin to feel more relaxed.

It's also soothing to know that this place is omnipresent: it's somewhere you can always reach when you need a few precious minutes of calm.

Exercise: Build Your Peaceful Palace

Now that you've gone through the guidelines, use this <u>exercise</u> to practice *building your own ideal environment.*

1.) Imagine a setting with all the trimmings: the scents, the right color, the right décor, etc. Make sure you take your time (at least 30 minutes). You want to get everything just right.

2.) Put the setting in place. Center it around yourself. What's to your right? What's to the left or there in front of you?

3.) Now imagine yourself actually in this setting, experiencing it and enjoying it.

- Were you able to actually live in that moment as if it was real? Explain.

- Does it make you feel calmer and more relaxed to use this setting? Explain.

Now that you've got this method down, let's move to the next one.

Chapter 3

Release All Negativities through Transference

Energy In The Palm

Albert Einstein said, "Energy cannot be created or destroyed, it can only be changed from one form to another."

Here is a calmness-inducing method that does exactly that. It's fairly common, and you've probably heard of it before. It consists of mentally **transferring negativity and tensions** out through the palm of your hand and into a pliable object, such as a ball, a sponge, even a piece of paper.

This method consists of actually connecting with those negative thoughts, then imagining them flowing out of you. From your mind, then to your arm, then into the pliable object where you crush them with one good squeeze.

Visualize it as if your worries were progressing through a maze. They're moving from your mind to your arm, then through the entrance (your wrist) and out to their final destination (the palm of your hand). After your palm, they escape into the pliable object and instantly get creamed, freeing you of them forever.

You can use this technique any time you're nervous before an event or a situation. An important meeting, an exam, or even a wedding if you need to.

Tension Transference Technique

Let's look at a practical use of this technique:

Instant Calmness

Before you get to your event, make sure you have a pliable object you can hang on to; however, if you don't have one, throw all your nervousness and worries together into one big, mental ball of energy instead. Make sure you give it a specific color (grey, red, rainbow-colored - it doesn't matter as long as you can visualize it with ease.)

1.) Identify every negative emotion you're feeling: fear, panic, uncertainty, uneasiness, etc. Watch them come together in front of your eyes in a distinct, colored ball.

2.) Watch the ball transfer first from your eyesight to your elbow (left or right, it doesn't matter), then, finally, to the palm of your hand.

3.) Now, when this ball reaches the palm of your hand, visualize it flowing into the paper ball (or whatever object you chose) that's actually in your hand. Now squeeze it. Feel all those worries being crushed under your own grip.

4.) Keep putting pressure on the ball for a few minutes (still visualizing your worries being reduced to nothing). If you're using a ball of paper to transfer your negative energy into, crush it, then toss it in the trashcan.

You should feel relieved and released of all your worries, and you should now be able to move on with life and your tasks for the day.

Learn to rely on this exercise and to use it whenever possible. It's easy and convenient, and the more you use it the more natural and instinctive it becomes.

<u>Exercise</u>: Negativity Demolition

It'll make it much easier to utilize the previous technique effectively if you practice connecting you mind to your vision. If you have trouble "seeing" mentally, all these methods aren't going to do you much good. But never fear, it *is* something that improves with practice.

Here's an <u>exercise</u> to help you do just that.

Sit down for about 5 minutes and concentrate on the various emotions that normally make you feel agitated and upset. You're going to want to learn to deal with a bunch of them at once, so pick about 5 to start with. If you prefer writing them down at first, go ahead. Now spend the next 60 seconds memorizing them.

> 1.) Once you've memorized them, imagine those words written in the air in front of you. As they appear, imagine them mixing and melting into one big red ball.
>
> 2.) Keep your eyes on the ball. Imagine it showing up on your shoulder, then move your eyes down your arm, your elbow, and your wrist, visualizing the ball being "dragged" along as you go. Make sure you have a sponge or paper ready in your hand.
>
> 3.) As it reaches your palm, imagine the red ball melting and running into the paper (or sponge,

whichever you have). Now *squeeze* as hard as you can. Imagine the red shattering into a million tiny pieces and blowing away in the wind.

4.) The key here is to put all the energy of your hand into the pliable object - as if all those negativities were entrapped in a building ready for demolition and your hand is the wrecking ball. Keep pressing until you feel that all the tensions have been demolished completely. At this point, you should feel considerably more relaxed.

- Were you able to successfully achieve this exercise? Explain.

Chapter 4
Pause the World Around You

Shutdown Mode

We all know about meditation and the benefits you're supposed to be able to gain from it. But what about all those times when you're too stressed to meditate effectively or you're in the middle of something you just can't drop?

Not to knock meditation or anything, but there are more versatile techniques you can use when you need a quick calming session. The one we're going to use here is as simple as **closing your eyes.**

Literally. *It's as simple as that.* All you have to do is close your eyes and put the world on hold for a few minutes. There really aren't any posture tricks or anything - all you have to do is let go. Let go of your present thoughts, and your entire body, and you can regain your calm in an instant.

This technique is the best one to use when you're feeling overwhelmed but you don't have time to utilize in-depth techniques that required more time.

- For example, if you work in an office, you can't just lie down any time you want and call it quits for the day. You're paid for your concentration and performance, so if you feel like you're losing it, this technique is a quick, effective way to regain your calm and keep going.

To use this method, try isolating yourself or finding a place where you can sit down and be undisturbed for just a few minutes. Once you're seated, release your arms alongside your body, letting your hands hang. Extend your feet out in front of you and close your eyes. Make sure your head is comfortably positioned and you can breathe freely.

Now, just let your mind shut down. Don't think about anything else, just the fact that you're closing down for a while. You're closing out the noise, the stress, the disturbing thoughts – anything and everything that raises your tension levels.

Ideally, this exercise should last for about 20 minutes, but if you're at work this could be longer than you have. That's okay. All that's necessary is to get your breathing stabilized, your mind cleared, and your body completely relaxed.

Think of it as shutting down your engine for a while. If your car motor starts giving you malfunction signs, what's the first thing you do? You shut it down and find the problem. Same thing here. When your brain starts sending you stress signals, it means you need to shut it down for a while and let it reboot.

Exercise: Letting Go

This method is based on "letting go." If you have a hard time putting that concept into practice, try using the following exercise.

> 1.) Stand up, looking straight in front of you, then slowly let your eyes close. After a few minutes, you'll start to feel almost dizzy or like you're about to faint. This is what you want. It means that you're body is starting to "shut down."
>
> 2.) Repeat the process, but this time perform it sitting down. Try it for 20 minutes (or however long you have to spare).

- What are your first observations? Do you feel more relaxed? Explain in a minimum of 150 words.

Chapter 5
Refresh and Stay Fresh

Get To Neutral

As mentioned from the beginning, you're not just learning to "deal with" stress and emotion, you're actually **exercising mental reflexes** that help you control your mood throughout the whole day.

This principle of "exercising" your mental reflexes is very similar to exercising physically. For instance, when you're about to begin an intense physical exercise, you generally want to stretch first in order to avoid injuring yourself.

It's the same when you exercise mentally. But in this case, mental "pre-exercises" can be applied to help you deal with the entire day or with an important but stressful event (a meeting, an interview, a test, etc.).

<u>Exercise</u>: Keep The Day At Bay

When you're just preparing for the day in general, you should add this exercise to your morning routine. You'll use it to start the day fresh, returning your mood to the "neutral zone."

You'll use this <u>exercise</u> to prepare your mind for the new day, leaving behind all stress about your job, your spouse, your children, etc.

This method basically works like the volume on a sound system. From a blaring setting of worries and preoccupation, you want to turn your volume all the way down: back to neutral.

1.) Stand in front of the mirror and look yourself in the eyes. Join your hands above your head and mentally say "-10." (This is the high point of your stress levels.) Now lower your hands by increments, mentally visualizing your levels moving up from -10 to level 0.

2.) When you reach level 0, (your hands should be about chest level) you can now open your eyes. Your mood should now be equal to 0 - as neutral as possible. Not happy or sad, simply neutral and calm.

3.) You are now ready to start your day (keep in mind that this ritual should last at least 5 minutes every morning).

Exercise: **Neutralize When Needed**

When you're faced with an important meeting or activity and you feel the tension starting to rise, you can proceed in the same way. But this time, take a little longer with the exercise.

1.) Find a spot where you can be alone for at least 15 minutes. You don't necessarily need to have a mirror, just repeat the previous exercise with your eyes closed. Start with your hands above your head (level -10), and keep going down. But this time, complete the exercise 3 times, making each session last about 5 minutes.

2.) This exercise lasts longer than the previous one because, rather than just facing the normal tensions of the day, you're now facing an immediate, important event and your stress levels are going to be considerably higher. Since this is the case, you're naturally going to have to work harder and longer in order to dispel them.

3.) After the third repeat, you should have gained better control of your emotions. This will give you the ability to face the coming ordeal with equanimity and calm.

*Have yourself practice this exercise constantly in order to improve your mind and mood reflexes. Once you can condition your mood and keep it to a neutral level (0), you'll be able to better withstand stressful ordeals and maintain self-control no matter what the situation.

Chapter 6

Calm Yourself

Exercise 1: Refresh Your Mood

In at least 150 words, and *using* your own words, can you define the concept of mood neutrality?

Using the technique illustrated, practice the 5 minute "mood refresher." When you've finished, try it again for 15 minutes (making sure you follow the guidelines properly).

- Were you able to reach level 0? Explain.

Exercise 2: Shutdown And Respite

When engulfed with feelings of moodiness, nervousness, impatience, etc., engage in a "shutdown mode" and take a short respite, writing down all your feelings and emotions before proceeding.

After you do this, take notes on your improvements. For instance: breathing calmly, mood is stabilized, more enthusiastic, etc.

Exercise 3: Environmental Takeover

1.) Using the guidelines for "creating your fortress of solitude," think of a place you hate to visit - one you always itch to get out of.

2.) What would you change to make it more welcoming? Write /type it down - be very explicit. Now come up with your own ideal setting. Don't forget to use as much detail as you can: scents, décor, colors - the whole deal.

3.) Next, close your eyes and imagine you're actually visiting this place. You've put a lot of work into this setting; make sure you take full advantage of it (*enjoy the moment!!*). Don't forget to relate to the scene as much as possible by imagining yourself actually hearing, smelling, and touching the objects you've included.

- Are you able to reproduce the experience or at least relive the soothing emotions every time you bring that place to mind? Explain.

<u>Exercise 4</u>: Goodbye Tension

1.) Once again, think about how you'd characterize your frustrations (fear, anguish, unrest, etc.). Pick at least 5 of them to make up your "tension ball" (follow the guidelines on transferring tension). Make sure you're armed with a pliable object.

2.) Practice giving the "tension ball" a color and moving it from one point to another (left - right, up - down, and so on).

3.) Now work on moving it to your elbow and from there into the pliable object in your hand (remember, the ball becomes or "seeps into" the pliable object in the process).

4.) As you visualize the ball becoming the pliable object, start squeezing to crush or release the tension.

- Can you feel the decrease in tension when you reach the last stage of the exercise? Explain.

Chapter 7
Peace Treaty with Yourself

Achieve Peace At Last

For people who are continually busy, the concept of "calm" is something close to unachievable. There's always something they need to be doing, something new for them to worry about and obsess over. If and when they start becoming control freaks, they're terrified of failure and uncertainty, experiencing countless nights of useless worry.

But endlessly stressing over your countless flaws and mistakes is the quickest way to send yourself into a spiraling meltdown. And though we might all think we know how to deal with this, we almost inevitably end up looking in the wrong direction to find the calm and emotional balance we need.

The truth is, you were born with your own ability to cope with all these stressors and to achieve calmness.

Maintain Peace

You just have to train yourself to deal with tension and stress.

To help you do this, just remember: you can't control everything in your external environment - nothing outside your sphere of influence is going to change just because *you* want it to. So take control of what you can: your mental reflexes and responses.

Take control of your mental environment, shut down every once in a while to let your mind recuperate, and learn to crush fear and uncertainty in the palm of your hand.

Because <u>calmness is achievable.</u> Calmness is something *you* can control with the tools you were given. You truly do have the ability to survive in this world and to move forward without all that crippling fear and doubt.

So don't wait for your yearly vacation in order to relax. Take control of calmness now!

Instant Calmness

An INSTANT Thank You!

Thank you for entrusting in the <u>INSTANT Series</u> to help you improve your life.

Our goal is simple, help you achieve instant results as fast as possible in the quickest amount of time. We hope we have done our job, and you have gotten a ton of value.

If you are in any way, shape, or form, dissatisfied, then please we encourage you to get refunded for your purchase because we only want our readers to be happy.

If, *on the other hand*, you've enjoyed it, if you can kindly leave us a review on where you have purchased this book, that would mean a lot.

What is there to do now?

Simple! Head over to http://www.instantseries.com, and sign up for our **newsletter** to stay up-to-date with the latest instant developments *(if you haven't done so already)*.

Be sure to check other books in the INSTANT Series. If there is something you like to be added, be sure to let us know for as always we love your feedback.

Yes, we're on **social medias**. *Don't forget to follow us!*

https://www.facebook.com/InstantSeries

https://twitter.com/InstantSeries

https://plus.google.com/+Instantseries

Thank you, and wish you all the best!
- *The INSTANT Series Team*

Instant Calmness

Made in the USA
Columbia, SC
25 January 2019